For Girls!

Star Performer

Deborah Chancellor

QEB Publishing

Editor: Mandy Archer
Designer: Nikki Kenwood
Illustrator: Jessica Secheret

Copyright © QEB Publishing 2011

First published in the United States in 2011 by
QEB Publishing, Inc.
3 Wrigley, Suite A
Irvine, CA 92618

www.qed-publishing.co.uk

Library of Congress Cataloging-in-Publication Data

Chancellor, Deborah.
 Star performer / Deborah Chancellor.
   p. cm. -- (For girls!)
 Summary: "This guide for girls gives advice on creative performances, including singing and
songwriting, acting and playwriting, hot music tips, stories and poems, and staging a performance"--
Provided by publisher.
 Includes index.
 ISBN 978-1-60992-103-3 (library binding)
1. Performing arts--Vocational guidance--Juvenile literature. 2. Women in the performing arts--
Vocational guidance--Juvenile literature. 3. Women--Vocational guidance--Juvenile literature. I. Title.
 PN1580.C43 2012
 790.2023--dc22

                    2011008177

ISBN 978 1 60992 103 3

Printed in China

Picture credits
(t=top, b=bottom, l=left, r=right, c=center, fc=front cover)
Rex 6t OJO Images/Rex Features, 23b Burger/Phanie/Rex Features; **Shutterstock** 4 blue67design and
azzzya (spot art), 4bl kavione and loriklaszlo, 5tr Valua Vitaly, 6c IQ Advertising, 6b CCallanan and val
lawless, 7t Mandy Godbehear, 7cl S1001 and keellla, 7cr Miguel Angel Salinas Salinas, 8 Irina Nartova
(spot arts), 8t Sparkling Moments Photography, 8b Juriah Mosin, 9b OJO Images/Rex Features and
lavitrei, 10 Nowik (spot art), 10c Sandi67, 10b Jarp2, 11t 89studio, 11br Aleksandr Kurganov, 11bc Wolfe
Larry, 13r Nikolay Moroz, 14t Poznyakov, 15r alexcoolok, 15b Ulrich Willmünder, 16b Piotr Marcinski,
17c Aleksandar Todorovic, 17b Tatiana Popova, Ton Lammerts, Picsfive, xjbxjhxm123, Tom Konestabo,
18b Alex Zabusik, 19cl Ladybuggy, 19cr Cheryl Casey, 20cr April Turner, 20cl deedl, 20cl cs333, 20br
Catalin Petolea, 21t Ingvar Bjork, Creative Illus, John Kasawa, 22t Jack Qi, 24br Booka, 26b Monkey
Business Images, 27c notkoo, 27r Andrey Klepikov, 27b Fernando Blanco Calzada, 28c Ariwasabi, 28b
Dan Gerber, 29l Sergey Lazarev, 29c Miguel Angel Salinas Salinas.

Contents

Sing Out!

It's easy to show off your musical talent—just open your mouth and sing! Singing every day is very good for you and will always put you in a happy mood.

Getting Started

The most talented singers treat their voices like precious musical instruments. Warm up gently, don't strain as you sing, and remember to practice regularly. Even ten minutes a day will make a big difference!

Private Practice

Until you get the hang of it, you might prefer to practice on your own. Try singing in front of the mirror, using your hairbrush as a microphone! Take deep, even breaths so that you can hold the long notes for just the right time.

Look and Learn

Flick on your favorite music channel, then watch how the celebs sing their songs. Now join in, carefully copying their vocal style. If you can't remember all the lyrics, scribble them down in a notebook.

Listen to Me!

Top singers need an audience! If your pals won't listen to you, perform for your family. Pick a time when they're not too busy so they can give you an honest reaction. If all else fails, try serenading your pet!

Join Forces

Once you've got the basics, you're ready to start singing with a group of friends. Find a song you all know well, then try singing it a capella— this is a musical term for performing a song without any instruments!

Learn the Ropes

To be the best, you'll need expert help. Every top singer has a coach! When your next birthday comes around, ask your mom or dad if you can have singing lessons. If there's a choir or music club at school, sign up! It's a great place to improve your vocal skills.

Audition Tips:

- choose a song to suit your voice
- practice for the audition
- stand up straight
- flash a big smile
- introduce yourself
- project your voice clearly
- if you make a mistake, keep going!

Karaoke Star

Do you long to be a pop star, packing stadiums with hundreds of adoring fans? Grab a mic, put on your favorite tune, then start singing!

What Is Karaoke?

Karaoke is a fab pastime that started in Japan. It means performing your favorite songs to backing music. If you practice with a video or computer game, the lyrics come up on screen as you sing.

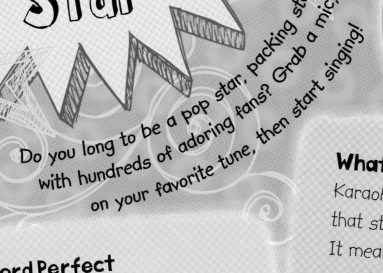

Word Perfect

Choose a hit that you can rock out to, then memorize the words. Once you've done this, you'll be free to concentrate on your dazzling performance rather than just getting the lyrics right.

Look the Part

When you've finished practicing, it's time to add a little sparkle! Dressing like a pop star can make you feel more confident—and this helps you sing better. Before you perform a karaoke number for your buddies, give yourself a cool celebrity makeover!

Rock Star Accessories

⭐ cool shades
⭐ hair jewels
⭐ neon leggings
⭐ bling rings
⭐ body glitter

Girl Power

If you feel a little shy about taking the mic, ask your friends to join in, too. There are so many amazing girl groups that you could sing along to. Work out a dance routine and split up the lines so that you all get to take equal turns.

Show the World

When you're happy with your karaoke performance, get a friend to video you. Download the movie, grab some snacks, then relax and enjoy the show—there's bound to be a bunch of laughs as you watch yourselves on screen!

Karaoke Sleepover

If your friends are as karaoke crazy as you, invite them to a special singing sleepover. Put invites in CD cases and ask your guests to come dressed as pop divas ready for a late-night show!

It's a Hit!

You're mad about music, so why not try composing a brand-new hit? Follow these songwriting tips and one day you could be number one in the download chart!

Remix

Composing can be daunting at first, so begin by writing new words to a song that you already know. Match your words to the mood of the tune—whether the track is sad, happy, or buzzing with energy.

Write a Rhyme

Listen again to the original song, then try to make your new words rhyme in the same places. That's not always as easy as it sounds! It might help to break the verses down line-by-line and practice singing new lyrics out loud.

Songbird

Now you're ready to compose a brand-new song of your own. Begin with the words—write a short poem about something that makes you laugh or cry. Repeat two or three of the best lines to make a chorus.

8

Melody Maker

Think about the spirit of your poem. Is it sassy, sorrowful, or sweet? Hum notes or experiment with a keyboard until you come up with a melody that suits this mood, repeating a section of it for the chorus or "bridge."

Two Become One

It's time to put your words and melody together! Don't panic if you don't know how to read or write music. Record your song, then play it to someone who can write down the notation on paper for you.

Funky Song Themes
girl power
feeling blue
party, party
I miss you
in my dreams

Première Performance

Work and rework your song, putting your heart and soul into every note. Video yourself as you perform, trying out any new ideas that might make it better. When you're ready, perform it for your friends and family. Tell them it's a world première!

Dancing Feet

Do you get lost in music every time you step onto the dance floor? You're just the person to come up with a sizzling new routine!

Star Turns

Before you try to choreograph a routine from scratch, take a look at how the professionals do it. Watch your fave divas perform on TV, then practice their signature moves in front of a mirror.

Making Moves

Choose a song to dance to. Listen to the lyrics, then invent a set of eight steps that fit well with the music. Think about movements that will bring the song to life. Keep the moves simple so that you don't miss a beat.

No Limits

Don't forget that you can mix different dance styles together in the same performance. If you like ballet, ballroom, or tap, try incorporating some of those steps into your routine.

Never Forget

As soon as you stop dancing, record the moves you've built into your routine so far—it would be a shame to forget anything! Write down all the steps or invent symbols to stand for the different moves.

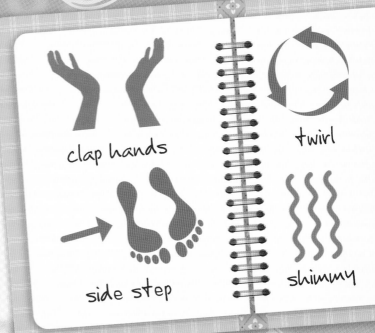

clap hands

twirl

side step

shimmy

Pass It On

Teach your pals the new dance routine. Don't expect them to pick it all up right away. Make sure they learn each section by heart before you go on to teach some more.

Strike a Pose

Before you wow your audience with a performance, decide what poses you and your dance troupe want to hold at the beginning and end of the song. This will add a lot of attitude and atmosphere to your routine!

You've Got Talent!

Putting on a talent show is a great way to get yourself and your pals up on stage! Recruit an organizing committee, then ask if you can host it at school. You'll have fun—and raise money for charity, too.

Tell the World

Make posters on your computer and put them up all around school, so everyone knows when the show is happening. Make it clear that contestants can entertain the audience in any way they choose—singing, dancing, telling jokes, or performing magic tricks!

Circle the Date

Ask your teacher to agree the date and time for the talent contest. Make it an evening so all your families and friends can come along. They may want to get on stage and perform, too!

MAY
18

Poster Checklist
- date
- time
- place
- entry fee
- name of charity

CALLING ALL RISING STARS!

TALENT SHOW
In the school auditorium
At 6p.m. on
Saturday May 18
Tickets $2
All proceeds to the school fundraiser

Get Your Act Together

So what about you? Do you want to enter the talent contest by yourself, as a solo act, or as part of a larger group? Don't let organizing the event stop you from showcasing your special talent, too!

Casting Call

Sign up your friends for the contest—and your family, too! Maybe your little brother is a whiz at impersonations, or your best friend is a brilliant violinist. Find out what everyone's hidden talents are, then persuade them to show off to an audience.

Try, Try, and Try Again

Learn your act, and rehearse it properly. Whatever you do, don't leave everything to the last minute. Try to work in a few surprises to make the audience remember you at voting time.

And the Winner Is…

Pick three people to be judges at the talent contest. Get the audience to vote on the winner, just like they do on TV. You could even make score cards for the judges to hold in the air!

Tall Tales

Are you a budding writer? Authors and playwrights get to share their ideas with readers all over the world! Use these tricks of the trade to improve your own unique writing style.

Bookworm

The best writers always have their nose in a book. When you read a story, you can learn for yourself what works well on the page. Reading helps you discover what kind of writer you want to be.

Different Stories

When you're ready to start writing, you need to decide what kind of story to tell. Think about the books you like to read and the subjects that you know a lot about. Maybe you're really into horses, or you had an amazing vacation that gives you a great location for a new tale?

Plan It Out

All stories need a clear beginning, middle, and end. Before you start, plan out the plot in a one-page summary, or synopsis. Grab your reader's attention, develop the action, then invent a nail-biting surprise ending.

Six of the Best

1. real-life drama
2. comedy
3. ghosts and ghouls
4. historical adventure
5. fantasy and magic
6. science fiction

Cast List

Great stories feature memorable characters who leap off the page. Decide who they'll be and imagine how they'd talk to each other. What are their names? Help your reader really get to know the characters by including a lot of dialogue in your story.

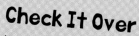

Check It Over

Every writer needs to go back to add extra details and make corrections. When you finish writing a story, you haven't really finished! Read through what you have written and make changes if you need to.

Key Change

Learn to type—you can pick up this skill by practicing on your PC or laptop. Handwrite your story, then type it up, so that you can make changes or add extra descriptions as you go.

Read Aloud!

There's nothing like a good story. If you want to write well, storytelling is a super way of developing your creative skills. Invite an audience to gather around, then lead them into the world of your imagination...

A Story to Tell

If you've written a story that you're proud of, don't hide it away—share it! Practice putting on voices for the different characters and run through any tricky words so that you don't slip up during the reading.

Test it Out

When you rehearse, try speaking in front of a mirror—that way you can experiment with gestures and faces that will bring the story to life. If you have a younger brother or sister, tell your story to them. See which parts they like, or find boring.

On the Edge of Your Seat

As you tell your story, you may decide to change some of it. Watch how your audience reacts—do they look scared during the spooky parts, and laugh when you want them to? Play with the volume and tone of your voice, until you get the reactions you hoped for.

Find Your Listeners

Who did you write your story for? Girls like you, or little kids? Ask at school if you can tell your story to children of the right age group. Speak clearly and try not to mumble. See how much they enjoy it!

Act Together

Grab some pals to help you tell your story. Ask them to act out the adventure as you narrate it—maybe they could take on the different character roles.

Changed Characters

If you're planning on performing to a big audience, find some costumes for yourself and your friends. If you can't find any good costumes, you could simply carry a different object for each role.

reporter

chef

pirate

gardener

maid

Poetry Princess

There are many kinds of poem. Some can make you laugh, while others are more serious. Poems often rhyme, but not always. See if you can write one yourself!

Funny Poems

Some poems are meant to make you laugh. They might be about silly subjects, or lines of complete nonsense filled with interesting, made-up words. Some poems get a giggle with clever rhymes, or surprise the reader with crazy endings.

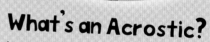

Poetry book

What's an Acrostic?

Poems can be laid out in all sorts of different ways. In an acrostic poem, the first letter of each line spells out a word. Can you write a poem like this, using all the letters of your name?

Hear the Beat

All poems have their own special rhythm. A lot of short words can speed up a poem, and longer words can slow it down. Not all poems rhyme, but all poems have a rhythm that you can clap out with your hands.

A Special Kind of Magic

If you want to write a poem, pick a subject that means a lot to you. It could be something happy or sad, or a message to someone you love. A poem is a very special, personal thing.

Please come to a poetry reading on Friday after school at Naomi's house.
RSVP
Tasty snacks and hot chocolate provided!

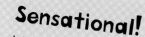

Sensational!

Use all your senses when you write a poem—don't forget to describe sights, sounds, smells, tastes, and sensations. Invent unusual comparisons to capture your reader's imagination.

Be Choosy

When you write, choose every word with care. Creating a poem is almost like making music—each word has an effect on the sound and feel of the piece. If you run out of words that feel right, check out an online rhyming dictionary or thesaurus for inspiration.

Drama Queen

Guess the Commercial

Divide your friends into teams. Get each team to pick a product then act out a commercial for it in under 30 seconds. The actor mustn't say what the commercial is for—it's up to their team to guess correctly.

If you need a bit more drama in your life, don't wait to join a stage school. Play some of these brilliant acting games with your friends.

Could you sell...?
- shampoo
- diamond rings
- dishwashing liquid
- dog food
- chewing gum

Scene of the Crime

Act out a crime scene news report with some pals. Decide who will be the reporter, police officer, witness, and victim of the crime. Get someone to video your news piece, so that you can watch it back on TV.

Impressive Improv!

Acting without a script is called improvisation. Dig out some random objects from around the house, such as a mop or a rolling pin. Take turns with your friends to act out a funny scene, using one of these things as a prop.

Pretend Party

Pick someone to pretend to be a party host, with the rest of you playing guests. Each of the guests should have an amazing but secret profession, such as an astronaut, brain surgeon, or champion dog trainer. During the scene the "host" has to question the guests until she guesses each person's special job.

Give Us a Clue

Pick a movie, book, or TV show, then act out its title, word by word, without uttering a sound. The person who shouts out the title first gets the next turn.

Feeling Moody

Pick a word to describe a mood, such as "excited," "overjoyed," or "angry." A friend can ask you to perform something in that mood, such as eating an apple. Can your friends guess what emotion you're trying to show?

Playtime

Were you born to perform? Do you dream of seeing your name in lights one day? Kick-start your stage career by writing your own play, starring you and your friends of course!

Get Inspired

There are many different types of drama—from children's shows to ancient Greek tragedies. Think about your favorite theater trips or watch some plays on DVD to get your creative juices flowing.

Work Together

If you're finding it tough to get started, try cowriting with a friend. Brainstorm together to see what you can come up with. Bounce off each other's ideas, inventing interesting plots and characters.

Every Good Script Needs a...

- dramatic entrance
- touching moment
- funny joke
- cool heroine
- shocking surprise
- bad guy to boo at

Perfect Parts

Count up how many friends want to be in your play so you can write parts for all of them. Try to give everyone a good-sized role, imagining what they might bring to each character.

Setting the Scene

Be realistic about the kind of show you can put on. It's better to produce a short piece really well than risk losing the audience's attention. Write a play that keeps the action in one place. It is difficult to make a lot of different stage sets.

Plot Spot

The secret of a good plot is to keep it simple. Don't bring in too many story lines, but keep the action moving. You could adapt an old story, or invent a new one. Write in plenty of twists and turns to keep your audience gripped.

Don't Be a Diva

If you work with a few friends on a play, there's bound to be the odd disagreement. Try to fix problems quickly and don't let anything get in the way of a great show! Make sure that even the quietest girl in the cast gets to have her say.

Stage Struck

You've finished writing your play—so what happens now? Cue rehearsals! Preparing for a production is a lot of work, but you'll all feel very proud when the curtain goes up on opening night!

Recruit Your Crew

Will you direct your play, or would you prefer to be on stage? You only need one director, but there are a bunch of other important jobs to do behind the scenes. If you're feeling shy, volunteer to work on costumes or paint the set.

Pick the Cast

It's up to the director to choose who plays which role. If a part was written specially for someone, they should be given it. You may need to hold auditions for the rest of the cast, picking the people who give the best readings on the day.

DIRECTOR

Learning Lines

Everyone involved in the play will need a script. Type the play and print out copies for everyone to take home. Ask your friends to highlight their own lines on the script, and set a deadline for learning them.

Go Slowly

Once everyone knows their roles, start rehearsing together. Begin with a whole cast read-through, then split into groups to act out each of the scenes. Bring everyone together for a full dress rehearsal just before the big day.

Pick a Venue

The venue for your play is crucial. Maybe one of your friends has a big backyard or living room that their parents will let you use. It might even be possible to get permission to perform your play at school.

Director's Job List

plan the scenes

tweak the script

coach the actors

practice the entrances and exits

check the running time

True Professional

Fix a date for the performance and work toward it. Ask a pal or family member to be your prompter. Agree times for all the rehearsals so the right cast members turn up when they're needed.

Look the Part

Good stagecraft adds pizzazz to any performance. It's all about getting the costumes, makeup, props, and sound effects right on the night!

Hair Affair

Practice all the hairstyles well before the final performance, so there are no last-minute disasters! To make a character's hair look right, you may need to use spray-on dye—always ask your parents first. If you want to wear wigs, browse in your local party store.

Costume Drama

Ask at home if you can borrow clothes and props for your production. Get your friends to do the same. You may need to go to thrift stores or yard sales to pick up some bargains that will suit the characters you are playing.

Magic Make-up

Actors can't go on stage without makeup. Practice with some face paints, enhancing your features so the audience can pick them out from a distance. Have fun, but don't overdo the colors!

Curtain Call

Check that there is space at the sides of your performing area for the cast to wait in between scenes. You could even decorate an old curtain to hang up at the front of the stage.

Handy Props
telephone
clock
hat and scarf
umbrella
walking cane
purse
camera

Prop Practice

Don't leave it too late to find or make props. You need time to rehearse with them. Remember not to use anything too fragile or precious as a prop, in case it gets broken or lost.

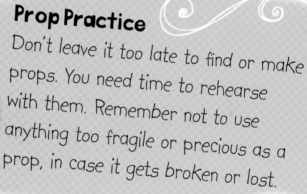

Sounds Good

Download sound effects and music onto your MP3, then burn them onto a CD. Put a friend in charge of the sound effects so that she's ready to flick on the tracks at all the right times.

On With the Show!

You've put a lot of time and energy into your play, now all you need is a good audience. Tell your friends and family about the show and spread the word about the hottest ticket in town!

Poster Publicity

Design a poster for your play. Don't forget to put on the title, plus the date, time, and place! Put up your posters well before the show so that no one misses out on your grand performance.

Souvenir Program

Take some photos of your friends at the dress rehearsal and ask them to write a short paragraph about themselves. Make a play program for the audience, adding the best photos next to each actor's biography. It will make a fantastic souvenir of the show.

Program checklist:
- title
- writer's name
- date of the performance
- intro to the play
- scenes
- cast list
- actor bios
- names of the backstage crew
- special thank-yous

Spread the Word

Tell everyone you know about the show so that you play to a full house. Ask your teachers if you can put a note in the school newsletter, too.

Shine a Light

Don't forget the lighting—perhaps your older brother or sister can help with this? A borrowed spotlight would add a lot of drama to the performance. Practice using lights at the dress rehearsal first.

Set the Scene

Before the performance, put out enough seats for the audience, and print plenty of programs. Select music to set the scene as the guests stream into the venue.

Audience Treat

Prepare snacks and drinks for the intermission and for after the play. The cast could even bake cupcakes or cookies to bring on the night. A few sweet treats are sure to get your audience clapping!

Star Performer Quiz

Are you a megastar in waiting? Grab some paper and write down the answers to this super showbiz quiz.

 1. **What is a great way to get better at singing?**
- **a** tell everyone how good you are
- **b** watch pop videos
- **c** practice singing every day

 2. **How can you improve the song you have written?**
- **a** sing it to your pet
- **b** video yourself singing the song then watch it back
- **c** you can't, because it's perfect already

 3. **If you want to invent a cool dance routine, you should:**
- **a** ask your dad for dance tips
- **b** mix and match your steps to the mood of the music
- **c** copy your favorite pop video

 4. **What's the most important thing about talent contests?**
- **a** taking part
- **b** showing off your skills
- **c** winning a prize

 5. **Good writers don't need to:**
- **a** plan the work
- **b** make corrections
- **c** worry about how good people think they are

6. All the best poetry has to:

a be imaginative and creative

b rhyme

c be set out in verses

7. What do actors do when they improvise?

a remember all their lines

b get stage fright

c act without reading from a script

8. How can you put on the best performance of your play?

a leave everything to the last minute

b get organized well before the day of the show

c don't worry—it will all be all right on the night

Look back at these pages: Sing Out! (pages 4-5); It's a Hit! (pages 8-9); Dancing Feet (pages 10-11); You've got Talent! (pages 12-13); Tall Tales (pages 14-15);); Poetry Princess (pages 18-19); Drama Queen (pages 20-21); Stage Struck (pages 24-25); Look the Part (pages 26-27)

How Well Did You Do?

Count your correct answers below to find out!

0-3 You've got a lot of confidence, but there's more to learn about getting your act just right. Don't give up—you'll be an accomplished performer in no time!

4-6 Not bad at all! You know what you're good at, and what you need to do to improve your skills. Keep going—you've got real talent!

7-8 Congratulations! If you keep going like this you'll be famous one day. Your charisma and creativity are infectious!

Index